Amazing Habitats

DESERTS

W

FRANKLIN WATTS
LONDON·SYDNEY

This edition first published in 2014
by Franklin Watts
338 Euston Road
London NW1 3BH

Franklin Watts Australia
Level 17/207 Kent Street
Sydney, NSW 2000

Copyright © 2014
Brown Bear Books Ltd

A CIP catalogue record for this book
is available from the British Library.

ISBN: 978-1-4451-3202-0

Dewey no. 577.5'4

Printed in China

Franklin Watts is a division of
Hachette Children's Books,
an Hachette UK company.
www.hachette.co.uk

Note to parents and teachers concerning
websites: In the book every effort has been
made by the Publishers to ensure that
websites are suitable for children, that they
are of the highest educational value, and that
they contain no inappropriate or offensive
material. However, because of the nature of
the Internet, it is impossible to guarantee that
the contents of these sites will not be altered.
We advise that Internet access is supervised
by a responsible adult.

Author: Tim Harris
Designer: Karen Perry
Picture Researcher: Clare Newman
Children's Publisher: Anne O'Daly
Design Manager: Keith Davis
Editorial Director: Lindsey Lowe

CONTENTS

•••••••••••➤

INTRODUCTION

In some parts of the world it hardly ever rains. These places are deserts. A place is a desert if it gets less than 25 centimetres (10 inches) of rain a year. There are some deserts where no rain falls for years.

SANDY, STONY OR ROCKY

The Namib Desert in southern Africa is a sandy desert. Not all deserts are sandy. There are also stony deserts and rocky deserts.

Ground squirrels live around the edges of the Sahara Desert in North Africa. They feed during the cooler parts of the day. At night they sleep in burrows.

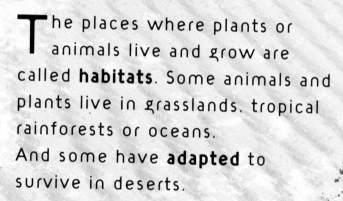

The places where plants or animals live and grow are called **habitats**. Some animals and plants live in grasslands, tropical rainforests or oceans. And some have **adapted** to survive in deserts.

Plants and animals that live in deserts have to be tough. Life is hard because there is so little water. It can be sizzling hot in the day and freezing cold at night.

Read on to find out what deserts are like – and how plants, animals and people survive in them.

Deserts of the

All deserts are very dry but every one is different. This map shows some of the things that can be found in the world's deserts.

The Joshua tree is one of the few trees that can live in the desert. It grows in the Mojave Desert in the United States.

NORTH AMERICA

SOUTH AMERICA

Llamas live in the Atacama Desert in Chile. People make clothes from llamas' warm wool.

Antarctica is the world's largest and coldest desert.

ANTARCTICA

World

Desert

The Gobi Desert in China and Mongolia is freezing cold in the winter.

EUROPE

ASIA

AFRICA

You can see the ruins of an ancient city called Petra in the Arabian Desert.

AUSTRALIA

Aboriginal people have lived in the Australian deserts for thousands of years.

CLIMATE

All deserts have one thing in common. They are very dry. Most of the Atacama Desert in Chile gets just 15 millimetres (0.6 inches) of rain a year. At one place in this desert it did not rain at all between 1903 and 1918.

DEATH VALLEY

Death Valley is not only very hot, it can also be very dangerous. In 1849, a group of 30 people took a shortcut through the valley. Twelve of them died from heat and dehydration.

Most deserts are sunny. They get very hot during the day. They are not hot all the time, though, and get much colder at night. Deserts in mountain areas get very cold in winter. Some deserts are icy all year round. Much of the frozen continent of Antarctica is a desert.

In winter, Antarctica is the coldest place on Earth.

WOW!
- The hottest recorded temperature in a desert was 56.7°C (134°F) in Death Valley, in the United States, in 1913.
- The coldest temperature was −89.2°C (−123°F) at Vostok, Antarctica, in 1983.

Wind and fog

Some deserts are very windy. Sometimes the wind blows strongly enough to lift dust and sand into a huge cloud, hundreds of metres tall. This is called a duststorm or sandstorm. In 2009 a duststorm started in a desert in Australia. It grew until it was 500 kilometres (310 miles) across. The storm lasted for two days and was so big it could be seen from space!

The Namib Desert is close to the shores of the Atlantic Ocean. It hardly ever rains there, but fog drifts across from the sea. Some plants and animals get all the water they need from the fog droplets.

SAND BLAST

The Mojave Desert in the United States is often very windy. The wind blasts grains of sand at rocks. This sculpts the rocks into strange shapes.

Cunning beetles

All animals and plants need water to survive. Some desert animals have surprising ways of getting water. Beetles in the Namib Desert, in southern Africa, stand on the sand with their back ends raised in the air. They catch tiny droplets of fog that is blown inland from the ocean. The tiny drops of water trickle into the beetles' mouths.

PLANTS

How can anything survive in a dry, scorching desert? Amazingly, there are many plants that can, from tiny 'living stones' the size of pebbles to giant cacti that grow three times taller than a giraffe.

QUIVER TREE

The quiver tree grows in southern Africa. It stores water in the soft, spongy wood inside its trunk and branches. Local hunters use the branches to make arrows.

All plants need light to grow, but desert plants have to survive in scorching sunlight. Daytime temperatures may soar above 30°C (86°F). At night they can plunge to freezing or below. Plants have to find water and hang on to it. They also have to protect themselves from hungry animals. Desert plants have all kinds of tricks to cope with these challenges.

This woodpecker lives in a hole in a cactus. Desert plants make good homes for animals that live in the desert.

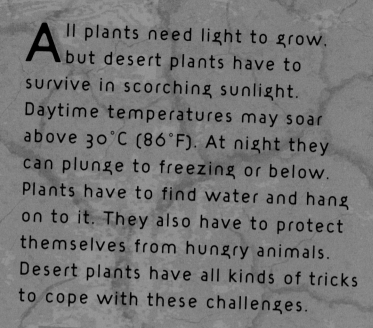

Old-Timers

Some of the oldest plants in the world live in the desert. *Welwitschia* plants (like the one above) grow in the Namib Desert. The oldest are up to 2,000 years old! They started growing in the time of the Roman Empire. The leaves of *Welwitschia* plants take in tiny drops of water from fog that the wind blows over them.

Leaves or spikes?

Plants need to store as much water as they can. Cacti plants have adapted to life in deserts. They have spikes instead of leaves, so very little water **evaporates** from them. Other desert plants are called **succulents**. They store water in their fat, juicy leaves.

For most of the year deserts are not colourful places, but every so often this changes. This happens in the Sonoran Desert, in Mexico, after it has rained. Then, seeds that have been buried in the ground spring into life. Green shoots pop out of the ground and colourful flowers bloom.

BIO FACT

Some plants that live in deserts ooze poisonous chemicals into the ground around them. The poison stops other plants, which will compete for water, from growing nearby.

'Living stones'

These stumpy, round plants look just like pebbles lying on the ground. If you take a closer look, you see that the stones are actually fat leaves. Their cunning disguise saves them from hungry animals. The plants, which are succulents, grow in the Namib Desert. The plants soak up water from the mist and fog that drift over the desert and store it in their leaves.

There are many saguaro cacti in the Sonoran Desert. Some grow very large – up to 14 metres (46 feet) tall. They tower over the desert. The water inside a large cactus weighs about 1 tonne (1.1 tons). That's as much as a small car. Saguaros can also live to a great age. Some are thought to be 150 years old.

Desert euphorbias are also succulents. They can survive in places where rain hardly ever falls.

ANIMALS

Most animals would not be able to survive in the desert. But a surprising number of animals do live there. Their bodies and lifestyles have adapted to cope with the tough conditions.

Life underground

Gila monsters are lizards that live in the Sonoran Desert. They spend most of their time in underground burrows. There, they keep cool to cut down water loss. When it does rain, the lizards leave their burrows to drink as much as they can. Then, they can go without drinking again for 90 days.

The ostrich is a flightless bird of African deserts and grasslands. It gets most of its water from the plants it eats.

There are very few trees in the desert where small animals can hide from **predators**. Many desert animals hide away in burrows in the ground for much of the time. The animals are usually sandy, brown or black. These colours help **camouflage** them from hungry predators.

BIG EARS

Like many desert **mammals**, the fennec fox has long ears. Large ears lose heat quickly, so help keep the animals cool in the hot sunshine.

Saving water

Desert animals can go without drinking for a long time. Camels can survive for several weeks. When they do drink, they can take in 118 litres (26 gallons) – that is more than a bathtub of water!

Hump stores energy-rich fats

Nostrils can be closed to keep out blowing sand

Gazelles that live in deserts, such as gerenuks in East Africa and dorcas gazelles in the Sahara Desert, never have to drink. They get all the water they need from the leaves and plant shoots they eat.

One hump or two?

There are two kinds of camels. The dromedary, or Arabian camel, has one hump (left). It lives in North Africa and the Middle East. The Bactrian camel has two humps and lives in Central Asia. Camels are sometimes called 'ships of the desert'. They carry goods and people across the 'seas' of sand. Camels can keep going for a long time without drinking or eating. That is because they store large amounts of energy-rich fats.

Large ears help to lose heat

Long legs help them flee from predators

Dorcas gazelles' pale sand-coloured fur gives them good camouflage from predators.

Ways to keep cool

To avoid the heat of the day, small desert animals often shelter under rocks or dig burrows. They may come out only at night, when it is cooler. Animals that only come out at night are called **nocturnal**. Nocturnal animals, such as the jerboa, leave their shelters mainly around dawn and dusk, when it is neither too hot nor too cold.

Jerboas live in deserts in North Africa and Arabia. During the heat of the day, they stay in their burrows.

Burrowing frogs

Spencer's burrowing frogs are amphibians – animals that need to live in water when they are young. Yet they live in deserts in Australia! Rain hardly ever falls. When it does, the frogs come out of their burrows to mate. The females lay their eggs in puddles. The eggs hatch into tadpoles, which grow into tiny frogs very quickly – before the puddles dry up. The froglets dig down into the desert sand and wait months for the next rainfall.

Desert predators

Burrows keep animals cool, and also protect them from predators. Bears, wolves, jackals and eagles hunt and kill mammals, small birds and snakes. Larger snakes and scorpions are also predators. They hunt smaller **prey** such as lizards, frogs and insects.

This rattlesnake is about to strike at its prey. Rattlesnakes live in the Mojave Desert. They hunt small mammals and birds.

The bark scorpion lives in deserts, where it eats insects and spiders. It tears them apart with its pincers or kills them with **venom**.

Pincers

Tail

Leg

21

PEOPLE

Can you imagine living in a desert? You would have to protect yourself against extreme temperatures. You would have to find food and water when both are in short supply. You might also have to deal with sandstorms.

CAMEL CARGO

In 1908, a line of 20,000 camels carried salt across the Sahara Desert. This was the biggest camel **caravan** ever. The days of huge caravans are gone, but desert people still use camels to move goods around.

Despite these problems, people have lived in deserts for thousands of years. They have learned to cope with the hard conditions. Some people are **nomads**, travelling from place to place.

Nomads move from camp to camp to hunt desert animals and gather wild plants. In the Sahara Desert, the Tuareg and Fulani peoples are nomads. So are many Aboriginal people in the deserts of Australia. Bedouin nomads have travelled the deserts of Arabia, Jordan and North Africa for thousands of years. Most Bedouins now live in cities but some still move around the desert.

Witchety grubs

The nut-flavoured witchety grub is a type of caterpillar. It burrows into the ground in deserts in Australia and later changes into a moth. Aboriginal people who live in the desert eat witchety grubs. They can be eaten raw or lightly cooked in hot ashes. They are a very healthy food.

Oasis life

Since ancient times, desert people have settled in oases close to where there are **springs**. Deep wells are dug to reach water far underground. With a regular supply of water for animals and crops, villages grew up. Some oases grew very large. The Al Hasa oasis in Saudi Arabia has 3 million palm trees, which are watered by more than 60 springs. Some oases have grown into cities.

Most people who live in hot deserts wear loose-fitting clothes that cover the whole body. These shade the skin from scorching sunshine. This Tuareg man is wearing a loose blue robe and a turban on his head.

Date palms grow around the lake at the Umm al-Maa oasis. This oasis is in the Sahara Desert.

Bedouin crafts

Most Bedouin people no longer live a nomadic lifestyle but have settled in towns and cities. However, they still carry out traditional crafts such as weaving carpets and making jewellery. Bedouin women have woven brightly coloured carpets and rugs for thousands of years. They often still weave on wooden looms, using yarn that comes from sheep's wool. Each tribe has its own traditional patterns and colours.

THE FUTURE

In the future, climate change will make some deserts bigger and others smaller. Some deserts might disappear completely.

SAND SPORTS

Adventurous desert sports are popular and will probably become more popular still. In California, people go 'dune-bashing' in desert buggies. Sand-boarding is another fun desert sport.

Irrigation channels supply water to parts of the Arizona desert. The watered areas have green crops but the desert is sand-coloured.

In some deserts, water drawn from deep underground has turned large areas into cropland or pasture for grazing animals. The desert is turning green! As the number of people in the world gets bigger, larger areas will be **irrigated**. More deserts will become cropland and pasture.

There are problems, too. More roads and cities will be built on some deserts. Other deserts will be dug up for the **minerals** buried beneath them. If people change deserts too much, plants may not be able to adapt and they could die out.

Quiz

Look at these pictures and see if you can answer the questions. The answers are on page 31.

1 Where in the world would you find these ancient ruins?

2 Are these 'living stones' fruits or leaves?

3 What is the name of this desert animal?

4 Witchety grubs are sometimes eaten by Aboriginal people in Australia. What does the grub grow into if it is not eaten?

Fact File

- About one-third of Earth's land surface is desert.
- The largest hot desert is the Sahara Desert, which stretches across North Africa from Morocco to Egypt.
- The biggest cold desert is the huge continent of Antarctica.
- Most deserts have a stony – not sandy – surface.

5 Do you know why parts of this desert are green?

Winners and losers

Crows have become more common in deserts because people have dumped more rubbish there, and the crows eat the rubbish.

Dama gazelles live in the Sahara Desert. Their numbers are getting smaller because people hunt them for food.

GLOSSARY

adapted: When a plant or animal has changed to help it cope better in its surroundings.

climate: Pattern of weather that happens in one place during an average year.

camouflage: A natural disguise that makes animals or plants look like their surroundings.

caravan: Line of animals and people travelling together through the desert.

dehydration: When a person or animal's body does not have enough water to keep working.

evaporates: To turn from water to gas when heated.

habitats: The places where plants or animals usually live and grow.

irrigated: Land that has been watered so crops can grow.

mammals: Animals, usually furry, that feed their young on milk. Camels, elephants, fennec foxes, gazelles, giraffes, llamas and ground squirrels are all mammals.

minerals: Rocks that are found in the ground. Useful minerals are mined. They include metal ores, salt and diamonds.

nocturnal: Animals that are most active at night.

nomads: People who travel around in search of food and water, instead of settling in one place.

oasis: Areas in the desert where there is enough water for plants to grow.

predators: Animals that hunt other animals, called prey, for food.

prey: Animals that are hunted by other animals, called predators.

reptile: Animals that usually have scaly skin and lay eggs. Gila monsters, snakes and turtles are reptiles.

species: A group of animals that look alike. Members of the same species can mate and produce young together.

springs: Places where water comes up from the ground.

succulents: Plants with fat leaves or stems that store water.

venom: A poison that some animals make in their bodies to attack prey or defend themselves.

FURTHER RESOURCES

Books

Calver, Paul and Reynolds, Toby.
Visual Explorers: Extreme Earth.
Franklin Watts (2015)

Gray, Leon. *Geographywise: Deserts.*
Wayland (2010)

Harvey, Gill. *Desert Adventures.*
Usborne (2013)

Newland, Sonya. *Saving Wildlife:
Desert Animals.* Franklin Watts (2014)

Websites

BBC Nature. This has beautiful
photographs of landscapes,
animals and plants from deserts
around the world, including
the Sahara, Australian, Atacama and
Death Valley deserts.
**www.bbc.co.uk/nature/habitats/
Deserts_and_xeric_shrublands**

Blue Planet Biomes. The animals,
plants, climate and geography
of the Mojave Desert in the
United States.
**www.blueplanetbiomes.org/
mojave_desert.htm**

Kids' World Travel Guide. Interesting
facts about the Namib Desert.
**www.kids-world-travel-guide.
com/namibia-facts.html**

LiveScience. The geography, climate
and animals of the Sahara Desert.
**www.livescience.com/23140-
sahara-desert.html**

WorldWide Fund for Nature. Photos,
videos, desert animals and plants
and conservation plans for the
world's deserts.
worldwildlife.org/habitats/deserts

Answers to the Quiz: **1** In the Arabian Desert. **2** Leaves. **3** A scorpion.
4 A moth. **5** They have been irrigated to grow crops.

INDEX